ED EMBERLEY'S
BIG RED WHITE AND BLUE
DRAWING BOOK

ED EMBERLEY'S
BIG RED WHITE AND BLUE
DRAWING BOOK

 LITTLE, BROWN AND COMPANY

New York ⌁ Boston

Little, Brown and Company

Time Warner Book Group

1271 Avenue of the Americas, New York, NY 10020

Visit our Web site at www.lb-kids.com

First Revised Paperback Edition 2005

Library of Congress Cataloging-in-Publication Data

Emberley, ED.

  Ed Emberley's Big Red Drawing Book.

  Summary: Presents step-by-step instructions for drawing people, animals, and objects using a minimum of line and circle combinations.

  1. Drawing — Technique — Juvenile Literature.

[1. Drawing — Technique] 1. Title 11. Big Red Drawing Book.

NC730.E64 1987   741.2′6   ■■■■■

ISBN 0-316-78974-7

10 9 8 7 6 5 4 3 2 1

WKT

Printed in China

THIS IS A WRITING ALPHABET.

ABCDEFGHIJKLMNOPQRSTUVWXYZ

YOU CAN USE IT TO MAKE WORDS.

CAT

THIS IS A DRAWING ALPHABET.

YOU CAN USE IT TO MAKE PICTURES

HERE'S HOW....THIS ROW SHOWS <u>WHAT</u> TO DRAW, THIS ROW SHOWS WHERE TO PUT IT.

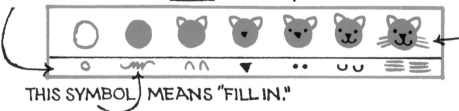

THIS SYMBOL) MEANS "FILL IN."

CAT

5

RED IS A JUST-RIGHT COLOR FOR DRAWING LOTS OF THINGS, SUCH AS :

RED ANTS, • MEASLES, CRANBERRIES, HOLLY BERRIES, CHECKERS,

CHERRY OR STRAWBERRY LOLLIPOPS, JAPANESE FLAGS, RED-CROSS FLAGS, DANGER FLAGS,

CHERRIES,

STRAW-BERRIES,

TOMATOES,

RADISHES,

APPLES,

TULIPS,

ROSES.

PINK

(LIGHT RED) IS A JUST-RIGHT COLOR FOR DRAWING A FEW THINGS

SUCH AS: BUBBLE GUM, CHEEKS, NOSES STRAWBERRY ICE CREAM,

 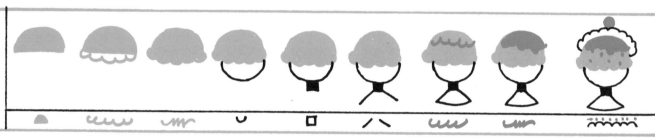

SUNDAE,

WATERMELON,

    ALSO

BUBBLE,

PINK ELEPHANT.

RED WHITE AND BLUE

ARE JUST-RIGHT COLORS FOR DRAWING AMERICAN AND OTHER FLAGS
AND THINGS SUCH AS:

FIRECRACKERS

ROCKETS,

ALSO

SWAGS, DRAPES, AND BUNTING.

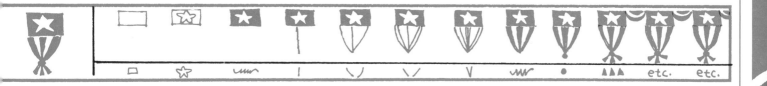

etc., etc., etc. ALSO ALSO

ALSO

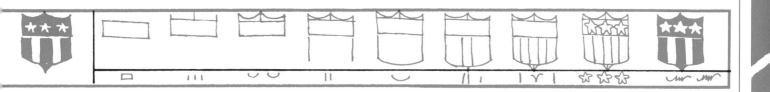

etc. etc.

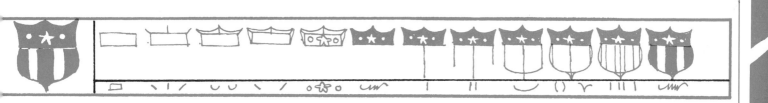

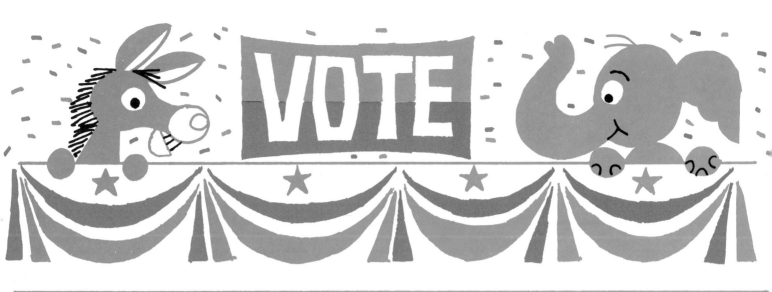

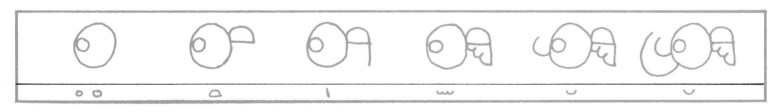

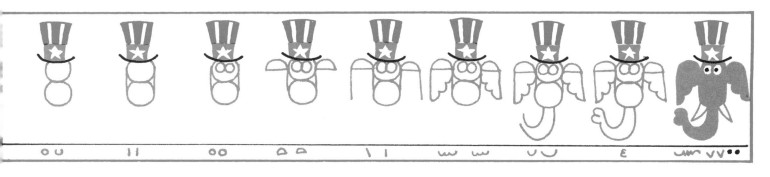

LIBERTY BELL

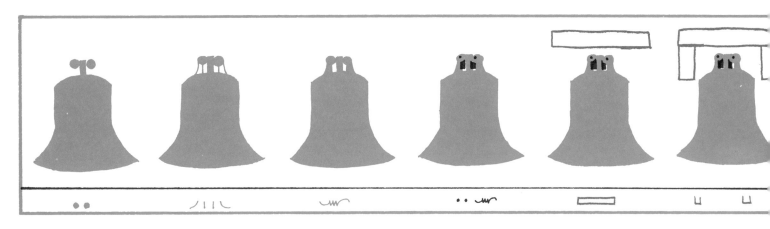

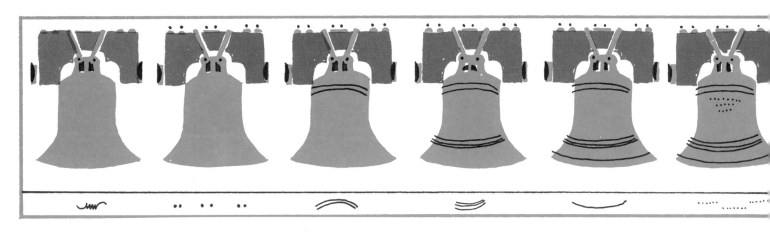

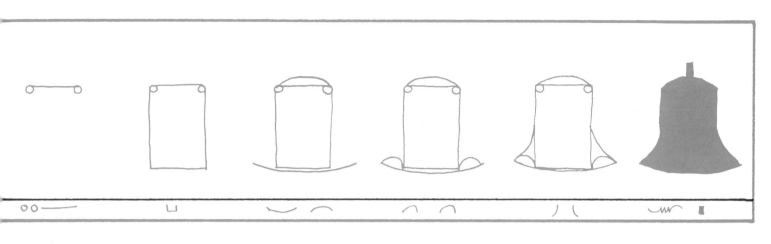

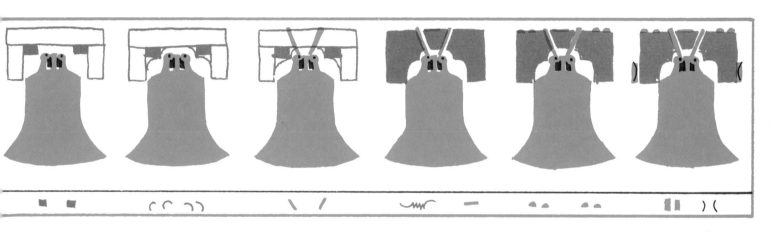

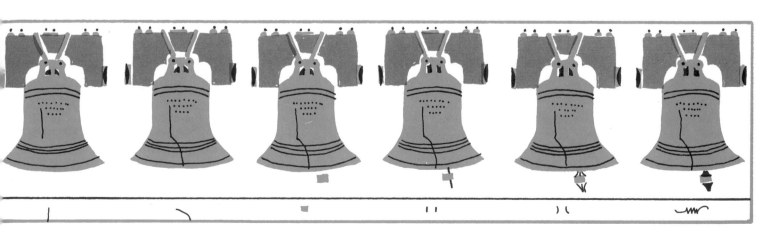

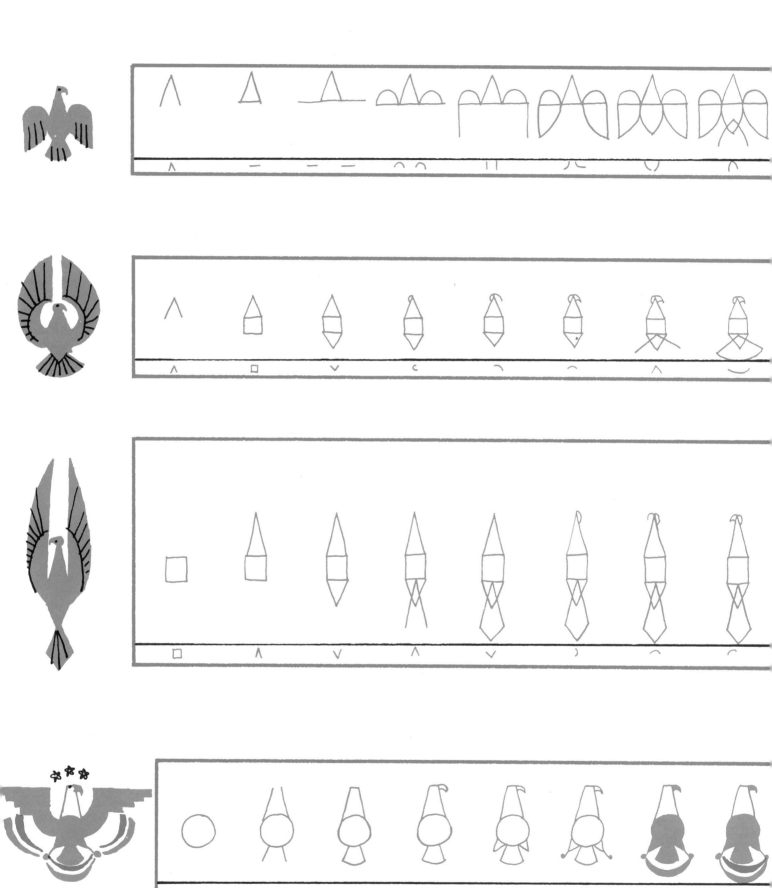

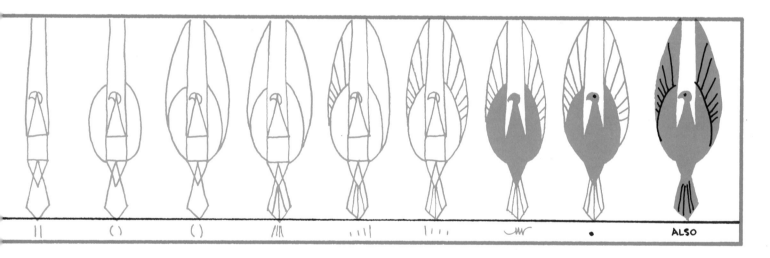

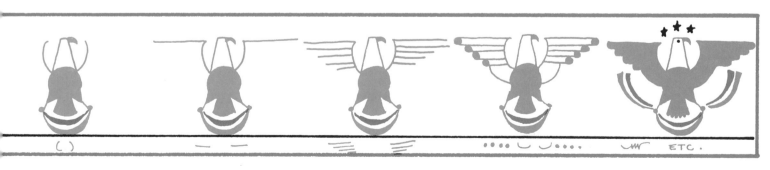

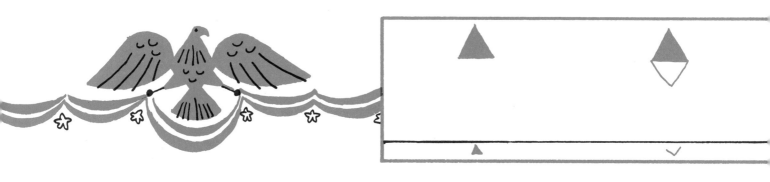

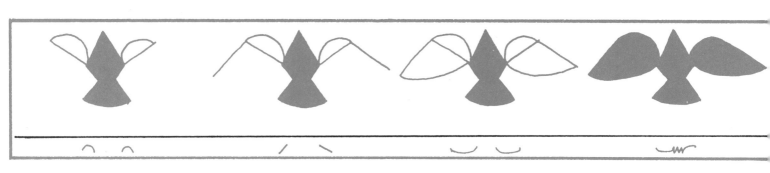

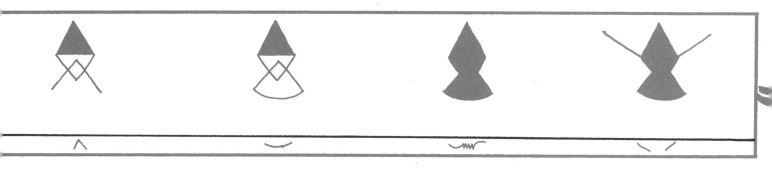

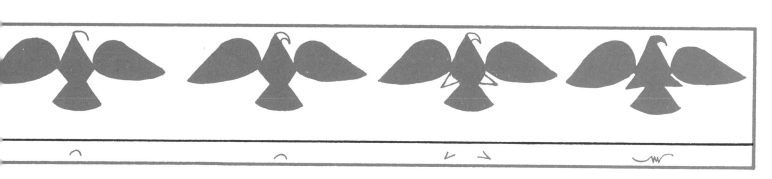

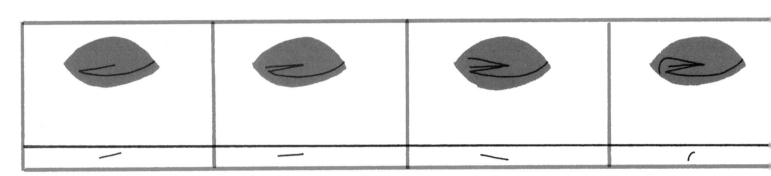

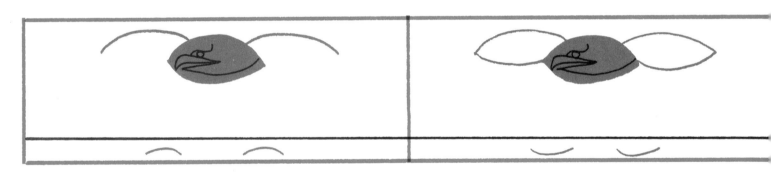

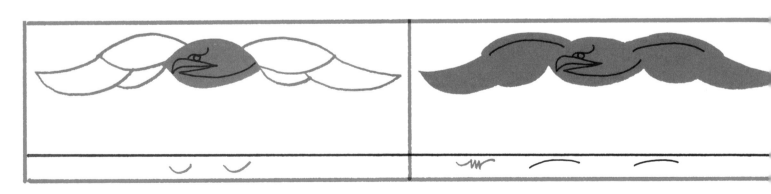

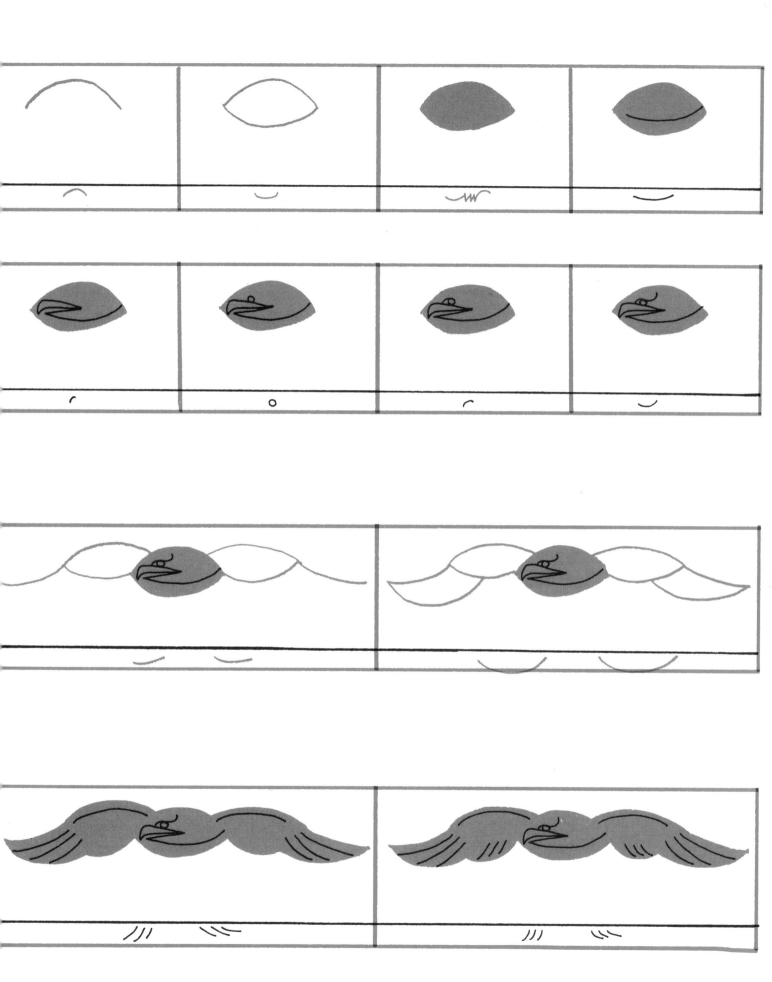

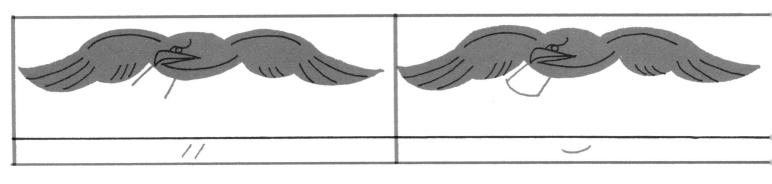

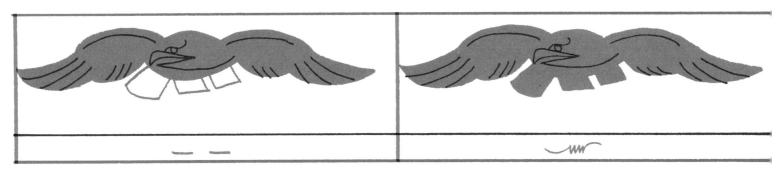

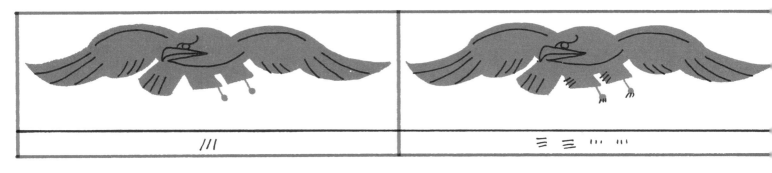

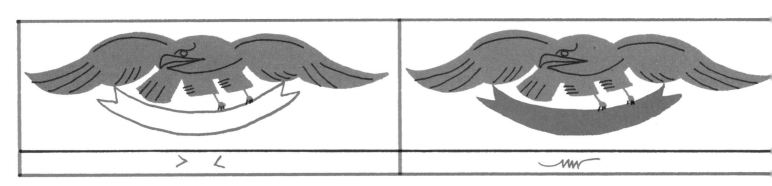

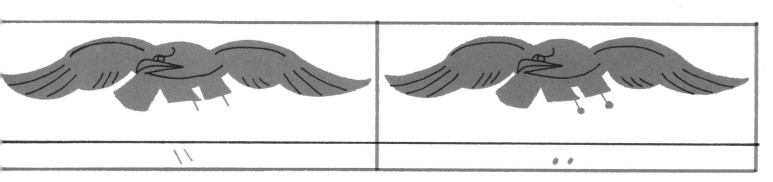

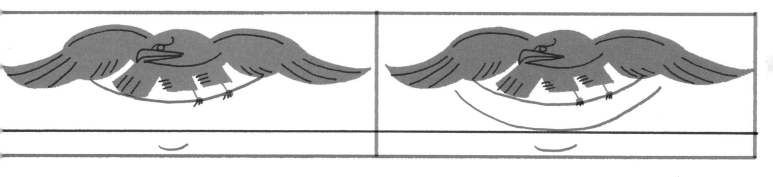

ALSO

ALSO

STARS AND STRIPES

FIRST, THE STRIPES, NOT <u>TOO</u> COMPLICATED. (13 STRIPES ∽ 7 RED, 6 WHITE)

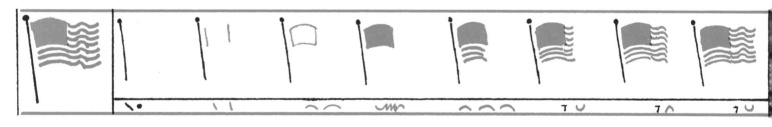

4 RED   3 RED

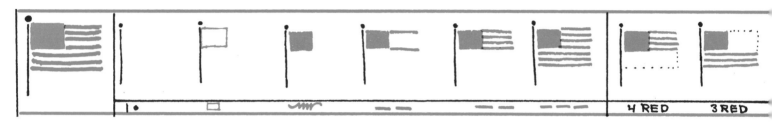

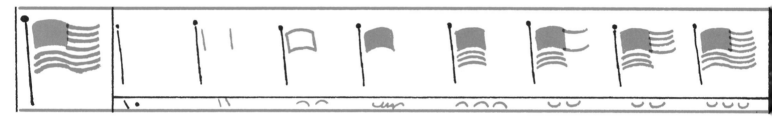

NEXT, THE STARS ☆ <u>COMPLICATED!</u> (50 STARS ∽ 5 HORIZONTAL ROWS OF 6 STARS, 4 HORIZONTAL ROWS OF 5 STARS)

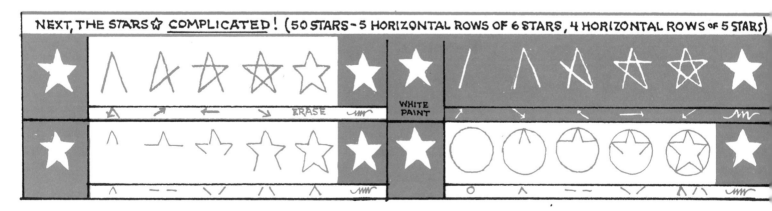

ERASE

WHITE PAINT

THE CANTON (THE BLUE RECTANGLE WITH ITS FULL SET OF 50 STARS)
FIRST, A SIMPLE METHOD, GOOD FOR DRAWING SMALL AND/OR FARAWAY FLAGS.

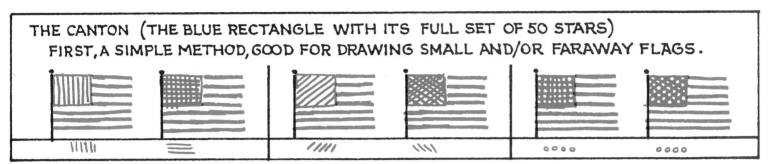

CANTON II   (FOR STAR COUNTERS)
    FOR DRAWING BIGGER AND/OR CLOSER FLAGS.

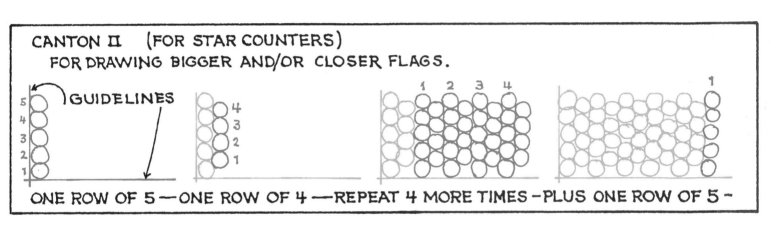

GUIDELINES

ONE ROW OF 5 — ONE ROW OF 4 — REPEAT 4 MORE TIMES — PLUS ONE ROW OF 5 ~

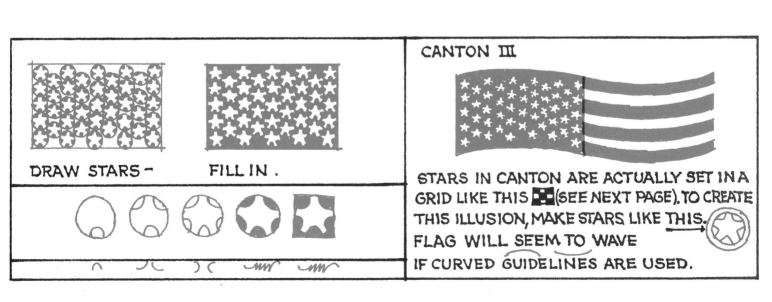

DRAW STARS ~   FILL IN .

CANTON III

STARS IN CANTON ARE ACTUALLY SET IN A
GRID LIKE THIS ▦ (SEE NEXT PAGE). TO CREATE
THIS ILLUSION, MAKE STARS LIKE THIS.
FLAG WILL SEEM TO WAVE
IF CURVED GUIDELINES ARE USED.

CANTON IV THE STARS IN THE CANTON ARE PLACED WITHIN A GRID THAT IS WIDER THAN IT IS HIGH. TO MAKE THIS SPECIAL GRID YOU MUST FIRST LEARN HOW TO "TIC AND TRY."

THE TOOLS — A "TIC STRIP" (ANY STRIP OF PAPER WITH ONE STRAIGHT EDGE.) A COMPASS, A TRIANGLE (OR AN OLD PAD BACK).

THE METHOD — "TIC AND TRY" IS A PRACTICAL, PROFESSIONAL METHOD THAT CAN BE USED TO DIVIDE A LINE INTO ANY NUMBER OF EQUAL PARTS, WITHOUT MATH!

FOR INSTANCE, HERE'S HOW TO DIVIDE THIS LINE INTO 3 EQUAL PARTS.

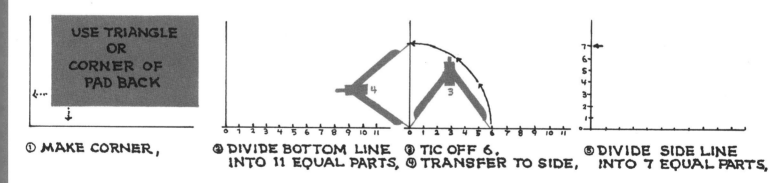

① GUESS ⅓ OF LINE
② TIC
③ TRY
④ IF NOT RIGHT...
⑤ GUESS AGAIN
⑥ TIC AGAIN
⑦ TRY AGAIN
⑧ KEEP TRYING
⑨ YOU <u>WILL</u> SUCCEED!

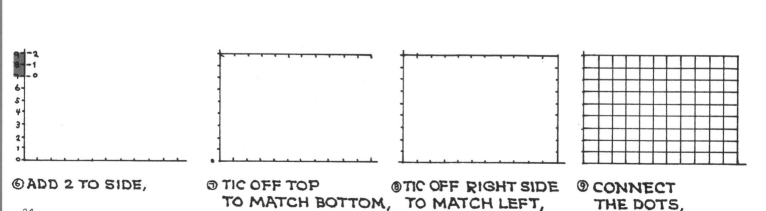

① MAKE CORNER,
④ DIVIDE BOTTOM LINE INTO 11 EQUAL PARTS,
③ TIC OFF 6,
④ TRANSFER TO SIDE,
⑤ DIVIDE SIDE LINE INTO 7 EQUAL PARTS,

⑥ ADD 2 TO SIDE,
⑦ TIC OFF TOP TO MATCH BOTTOM,
⑧ TIC OFF RIGHT SIDE TO MATCH LEFT,
⑨ CONNECT THE DOTS,

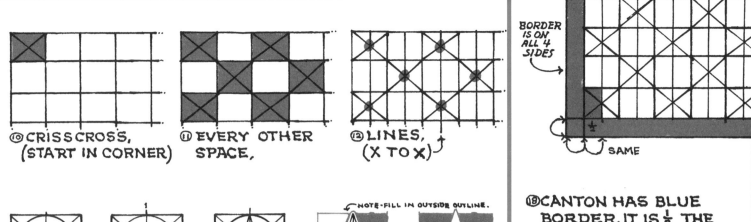

⑩ CRISS CROSS, (START IN CORNER)

⑪ EVERY OTHER SPACE,

⑫ LINES, (X TO X)

NOTE-FILL IN OUTSIDE OUTLINE.

⑬ CIRCLE, ⑭ DIVIDE, 5 PARTS ⑮ DOT-TO-DOT, ⑯ OUTLINE, ⑰ FILL, ERASE,

BORDER IS ON ALL 4 SIDES

SAME

⑱ CANTON HAS BLUE BORDER. IT IS ½ THE WIDTH OF A STAR SPACE

FOR MORE STAR TALK AND LARGE CANTON SEE NEXT PAGE →

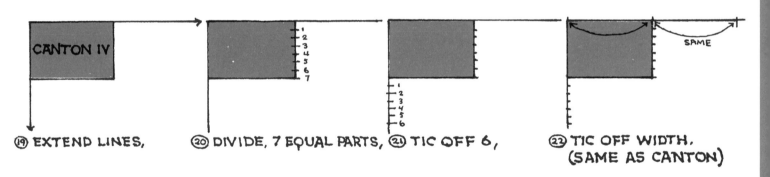

CANTON IV

⑲ EXTEND LINES,

⑳ DIVIDE, 7 EQUAL PARTS, ㉑ TIC OFF 6,

SAME

㉒ TIC OFF WIDTH, (SAME AS CANTON)

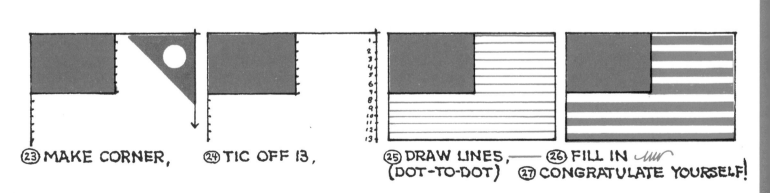

㉓ MAKE CORNER,

㉔ TIC OFF 13,

㉕ DRAW LINES, (DOT-TO-DOT)

㉖ FILL IN

㉗ CONGRATULATE YOURSELF!

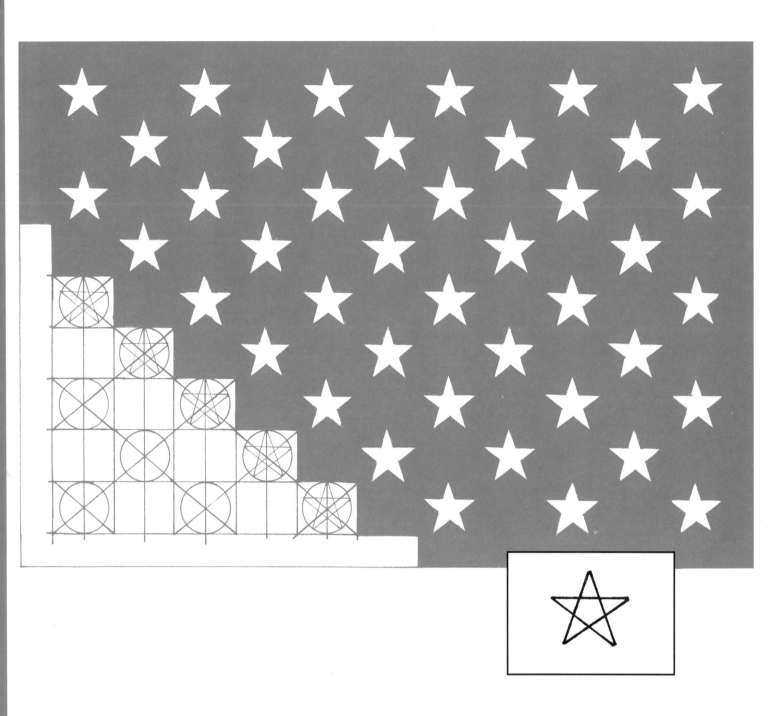

ACCURACY-DIFFICULT IN SMALL SIZES THE LARGER THE EASIER
CANTON Ⅴ-A FURTHER REFINEMENT, STAR POINTS SHOULD TOUCH
TOP AND BOTTOM OF STAR BOX (BUT NOT THE SIDES).

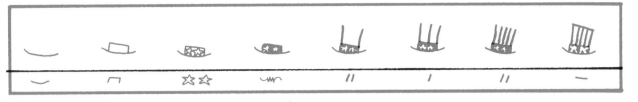

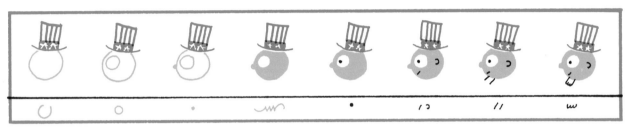

UNCLE
★SAM★

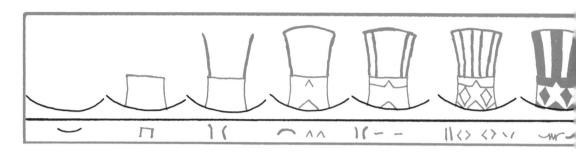

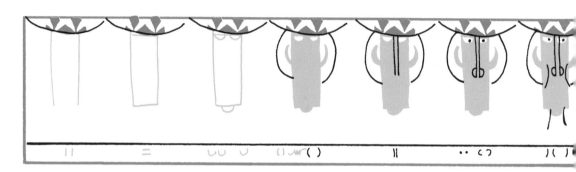

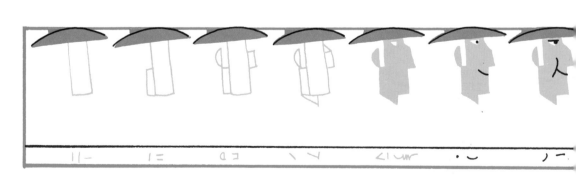

VALENTINE'S DAY

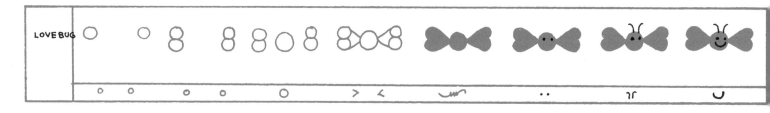

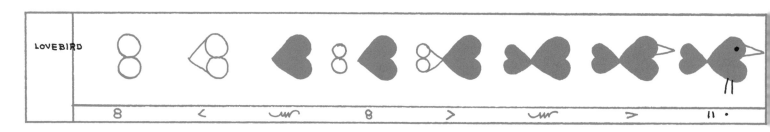

CUPID

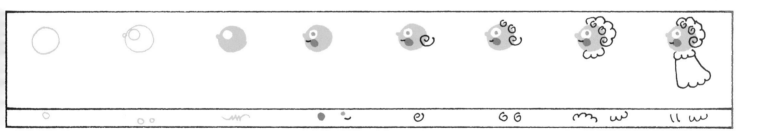

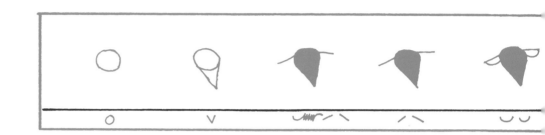

BLEEZYBUB and DEVIL DOG

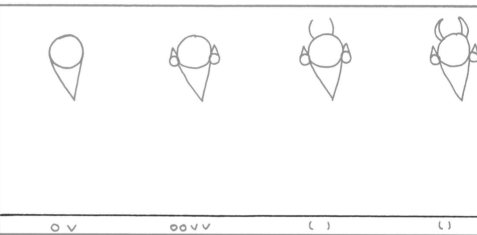

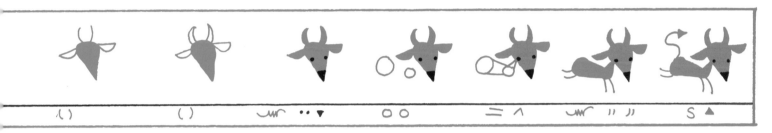

CARGO SHIPS

FREIGHTER / OCEAN-GOING SHIP, VARIOUS CARGOES.

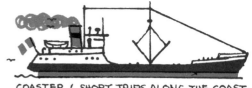

COASTER / SHORT TRIPS ALONG THE COAST

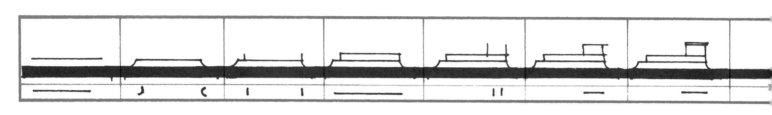

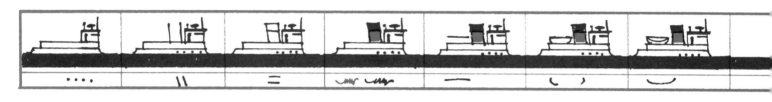

POOP DECK

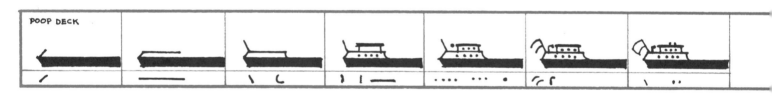

ALSO

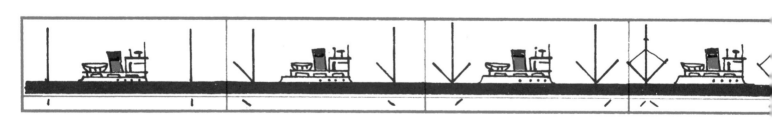

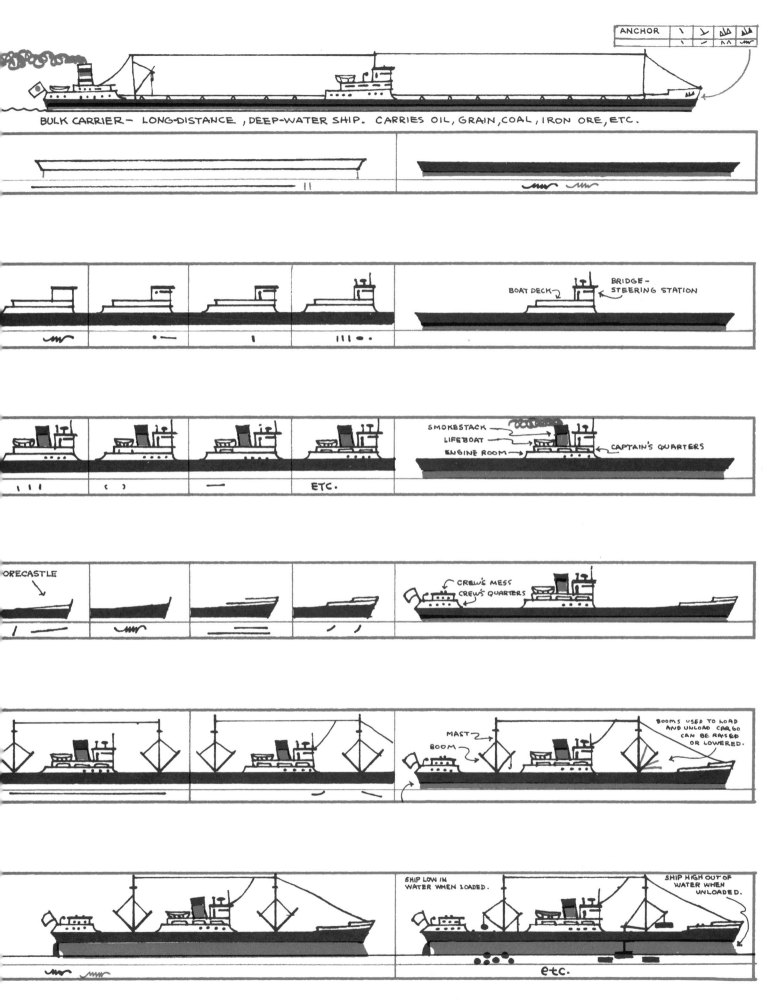

ANCHOR

BULK CARRIER — LONG-DISTANCE, DEEP-WATER SHIP. CARRIES OIL, GRAIN, COAL, IRON ORE, ETC.

BOAT DECK
BRIDGE — STEERING STATION

ETC.

SMOKESTACK
LIFEBOAT
ENGINE ROOM
CAPTAIN'S QUARTERS

FORECASTLE

CREW'S MESS
CREW'S QUARTERS

MAST
BOOM

BOOMS USED TO LOAD AND UNLOAD CARGO CAN BE RAISED OR LOWERED.

SHIP LOW IN WATER WHEN LOADED.

SHIP HIGH OUT OF WATER WHEN UNLOADED.

etc.

TUGBOAT

TUGBOATS ARE USED TO PUSH OR PULL OTHER BOATS, SHIPS, AND BARGES.

STAR TUG CO.

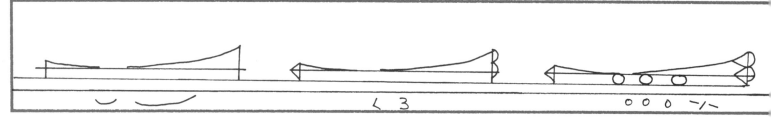

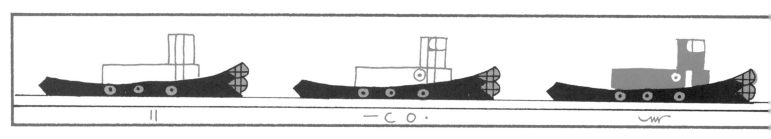

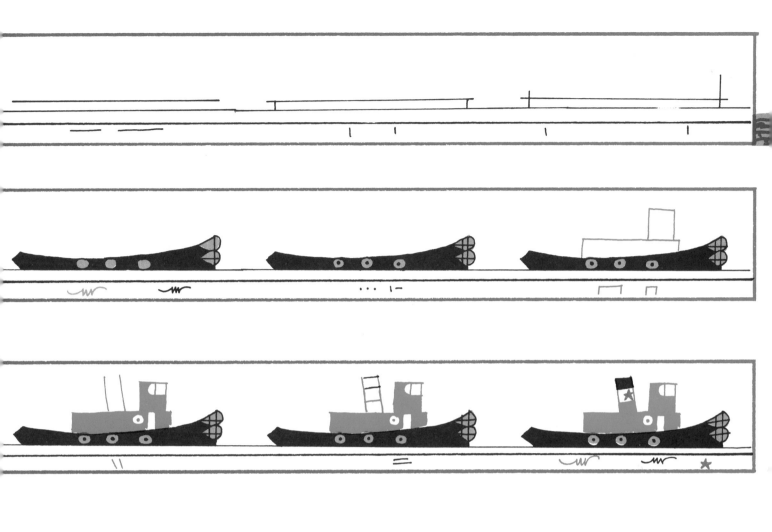

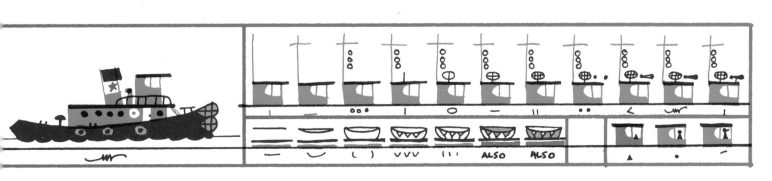

LIGHTSHIP

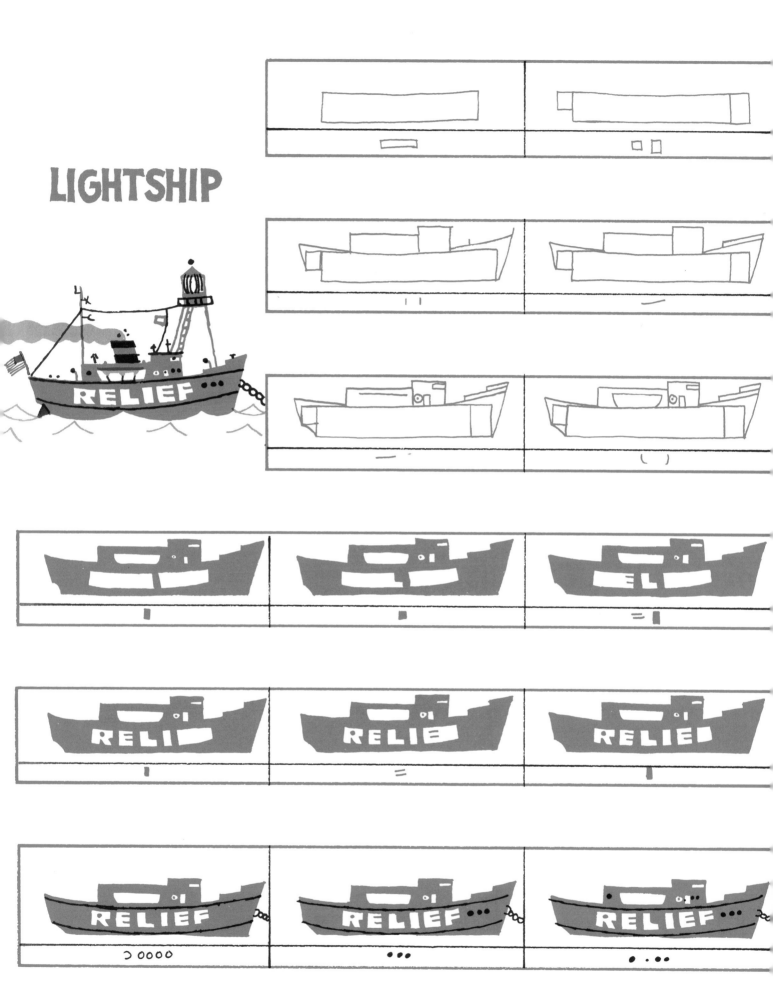

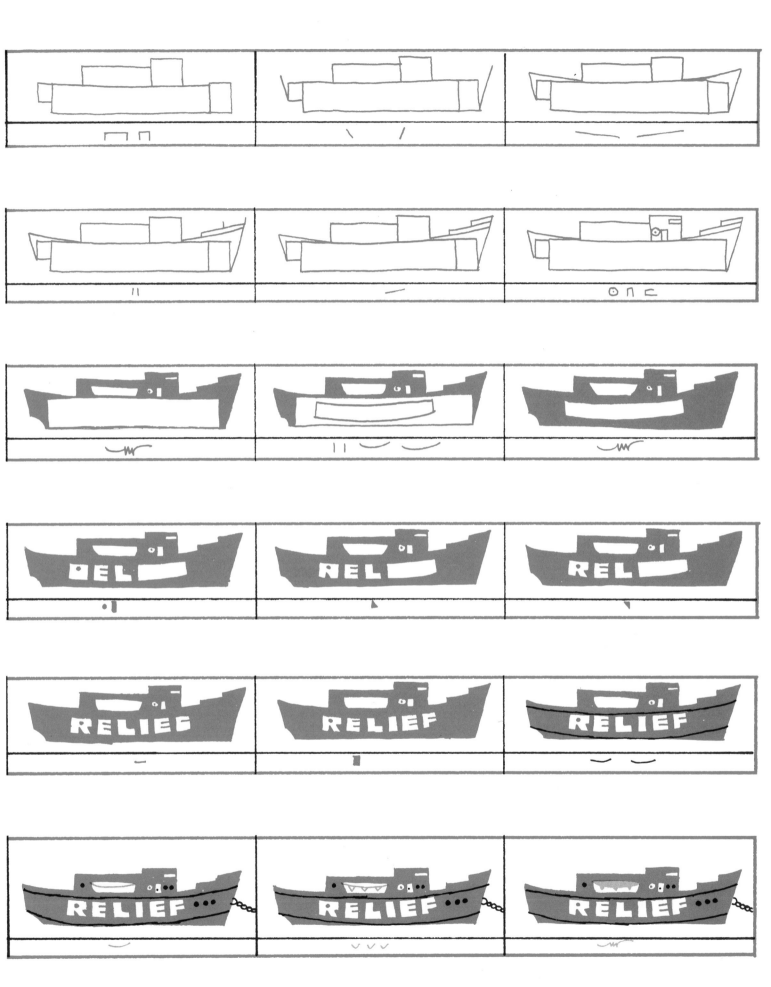

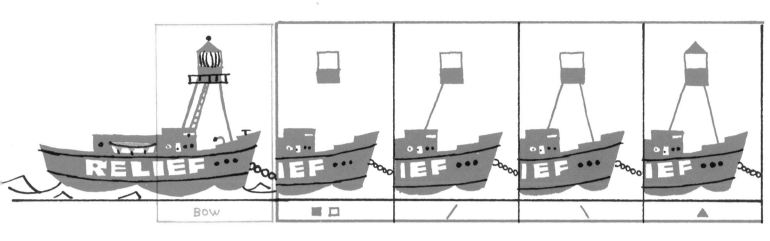

BOW

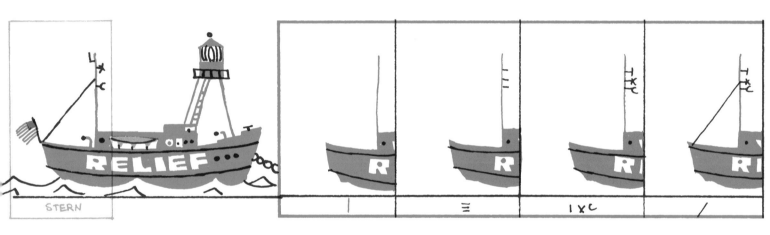

STERN

MIDSHIPS

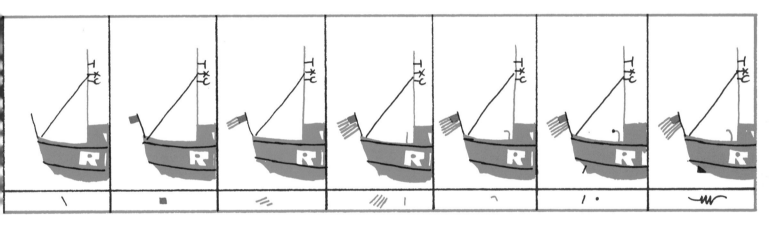

43

POLICE CRUISER

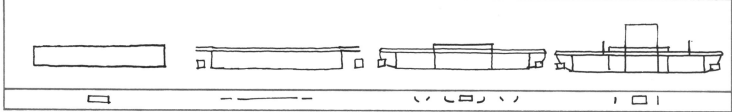

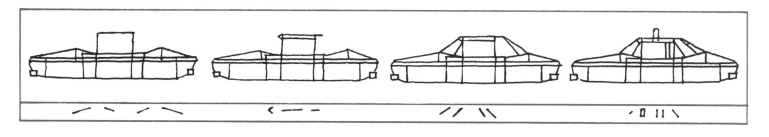

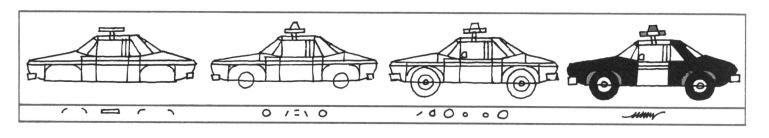

ETC.

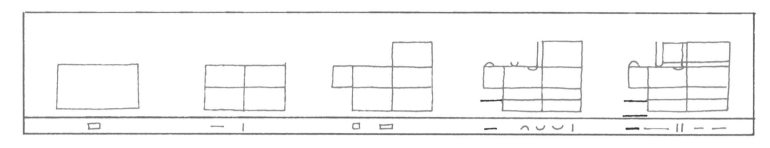

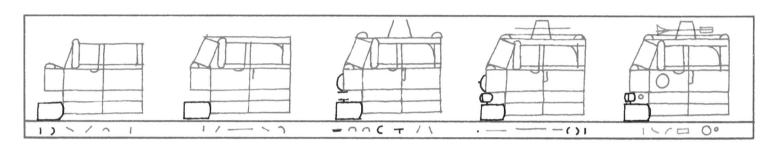

FIRE ENGINES

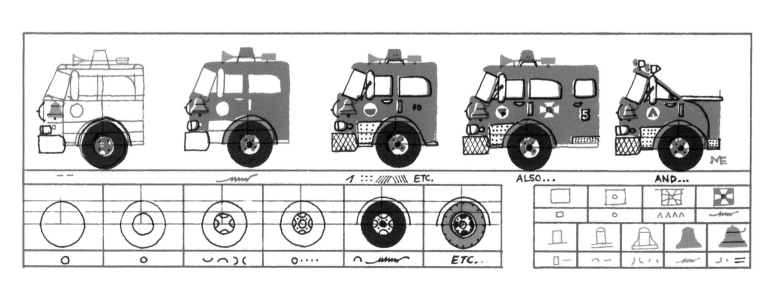

ETC.

ALSO...

AND...

ETC...

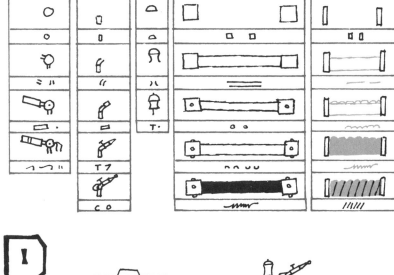

PUMPER

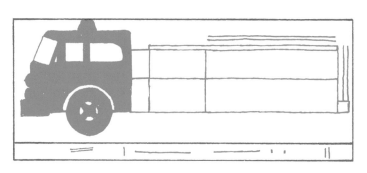

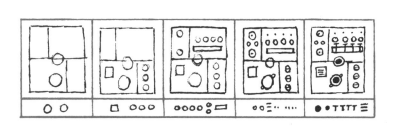

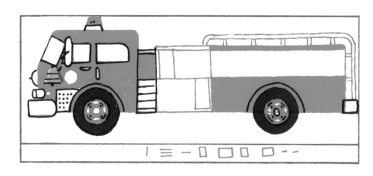

SNORKEL

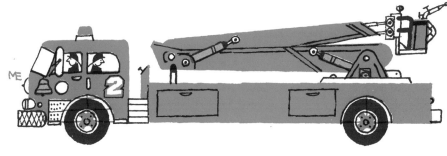

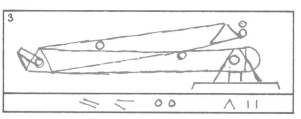

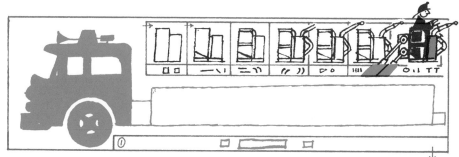

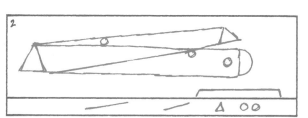

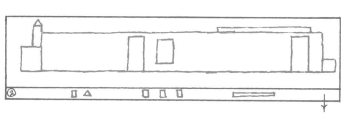

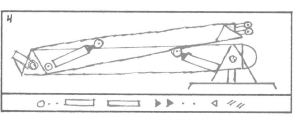

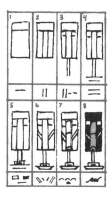

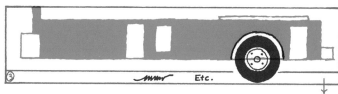

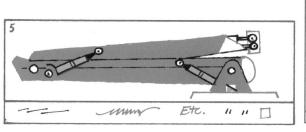

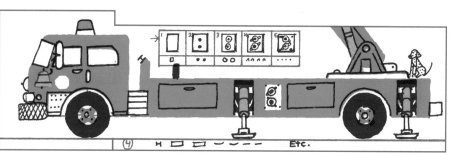

HOOK AND LADDER

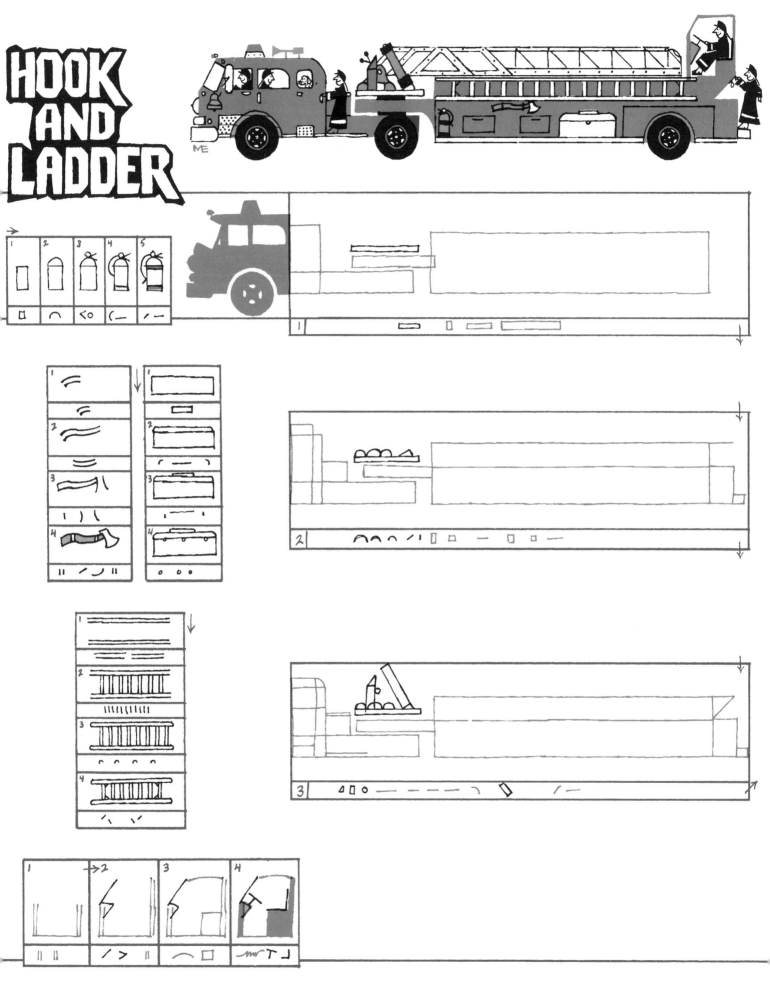

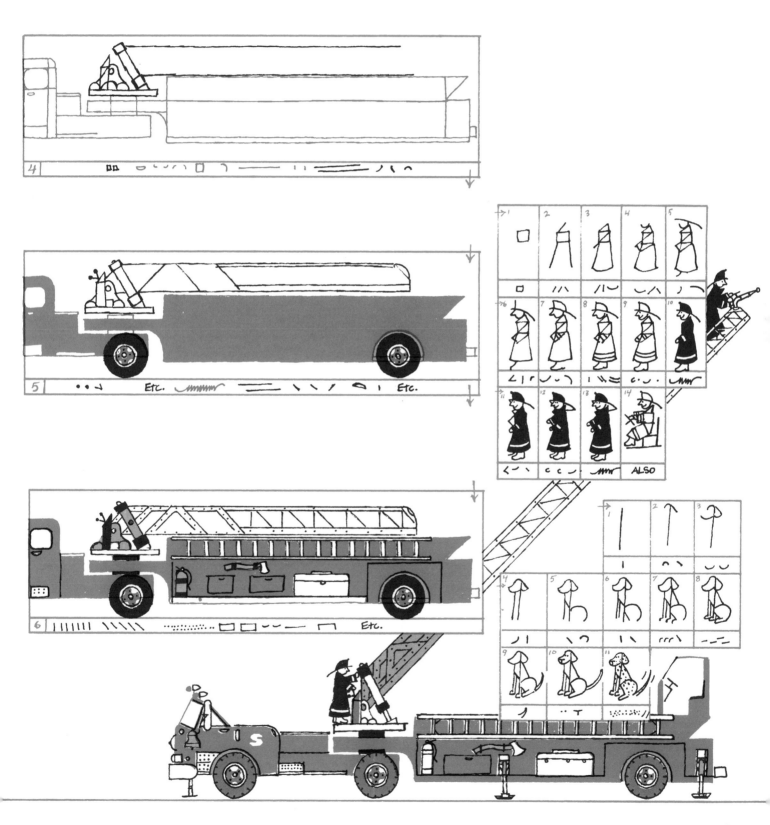

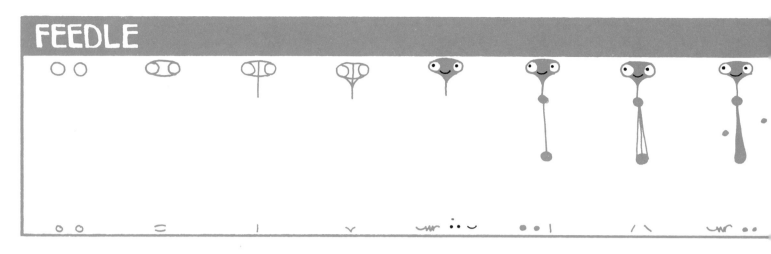

FOODLE AS SEEN FROM FEED

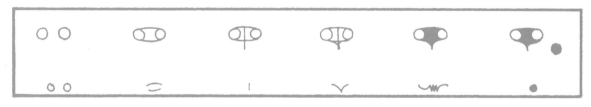

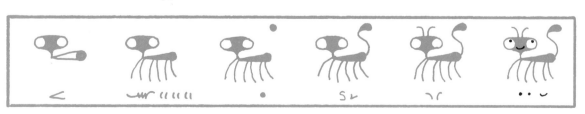

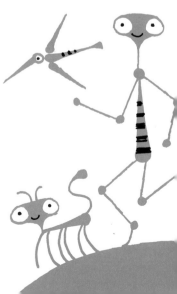

FEEDLE SPACESHIP
(NICKNAME..."THE FEEDLE NEEDLE")

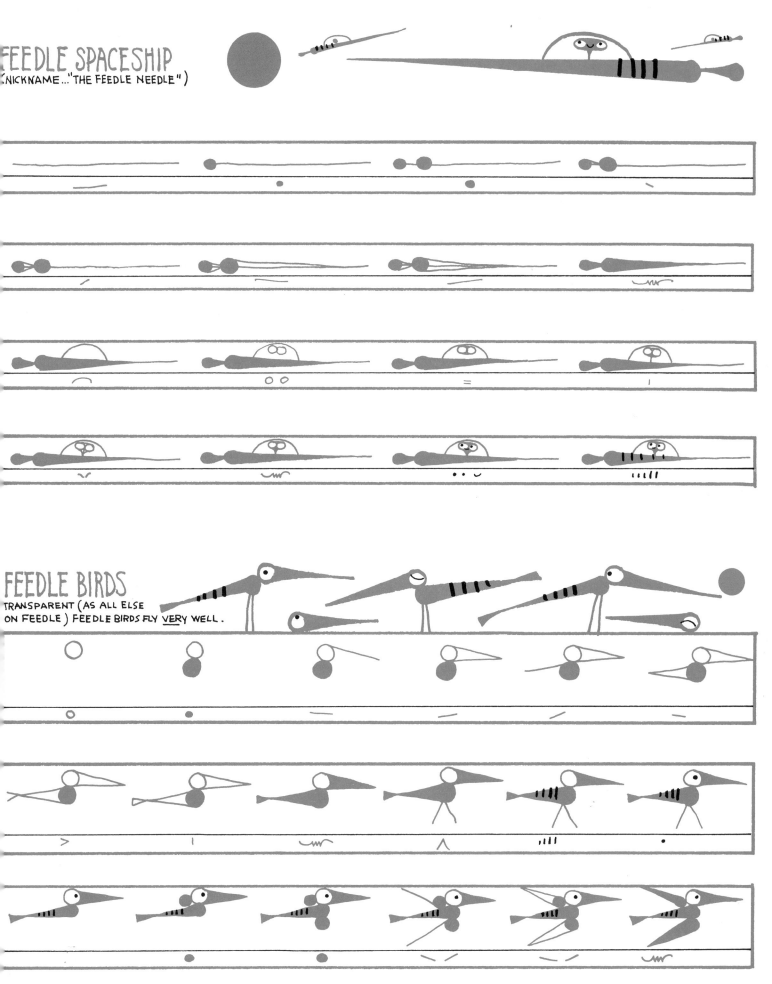

FEEDLE BIRDS
TRANSPARENT (AS ALL ELSE
ON FEEDLE) FEEDLE BIRDS FLY VERY WELL.

FOODLE

FOODLE AND FEEDLE ARE THE TWIN MOONS OF PLANET ZORT. (ZORT IN <u>BIG GREEN DRAWING BOOK.</u>)

FOODLER

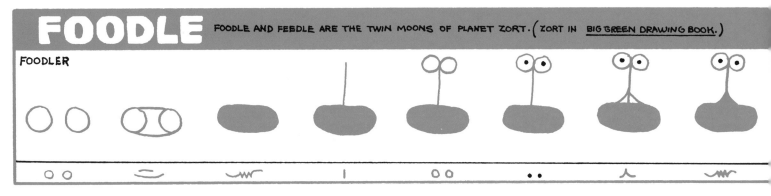

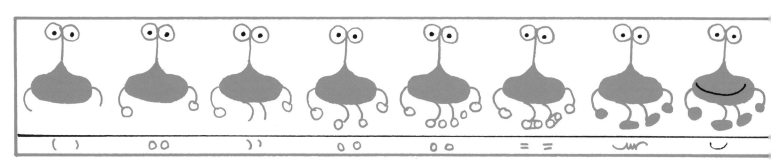

FEEDLE AS SEEN FROM FOODLE

FOODLE PET

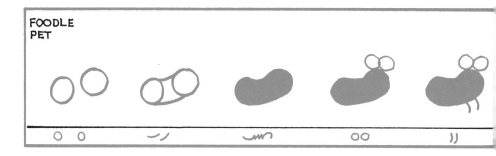

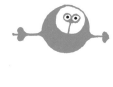

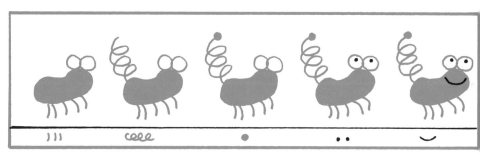

FOODLE SPACESHIP

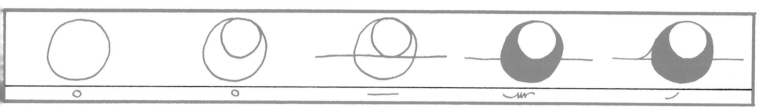

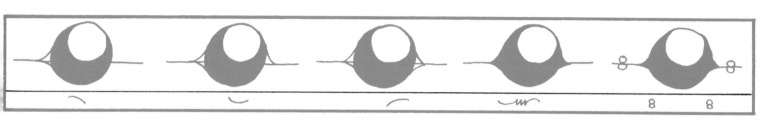

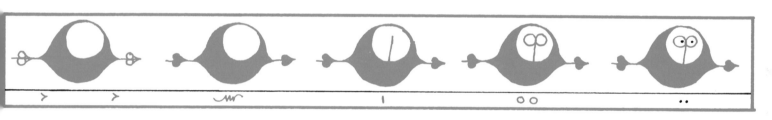

FOODLE BIRDS

FOODLE BIRDS DO NOT FLY.
(THEY HAVE NO WINGS)

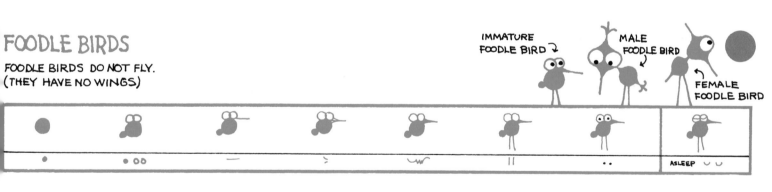

IMMATURE FOODLE BIRD

MALE FOODLE BIRD

FEMALE FOODLE BIRD

ASLEEP

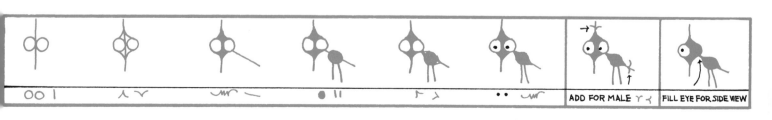

ADD FOR MALE

FILL EYE FOR SIDE VIEW

PATCHES (THE SCARECROW) AND THE "ISH" BIRDS

ETC.

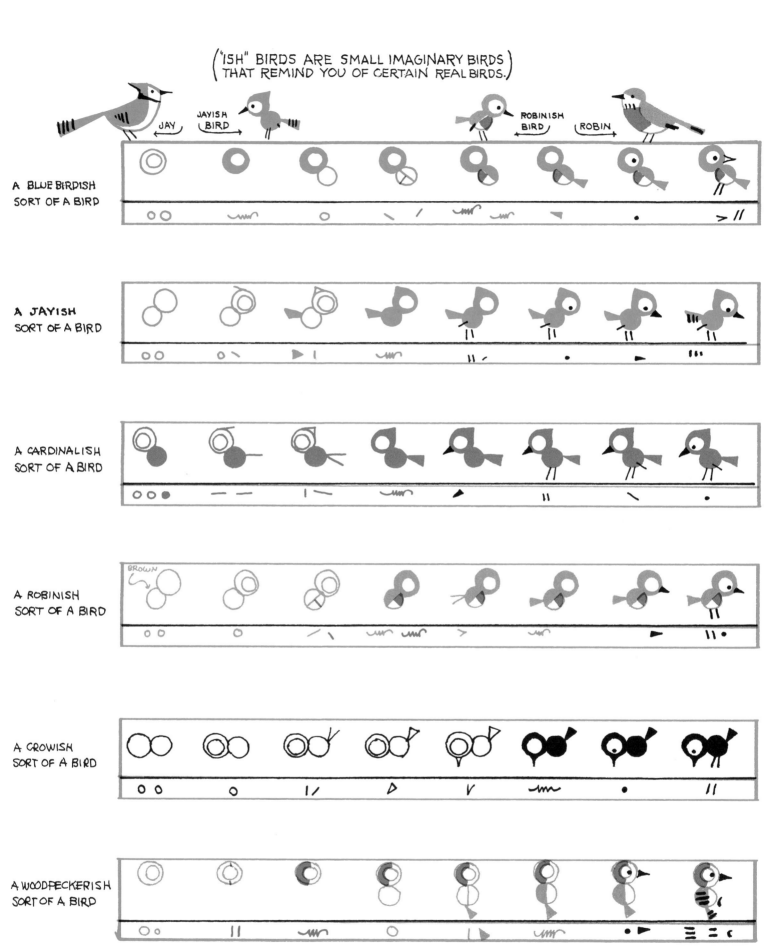

("ISH" BIRDS ARE SMALL IMAGINARY BIRDS
THAT REMIND YOU OF CERTAIN REAL BIRDS.)

JAY   JAYISH BIRD   ROBINISH BIRD   ROBIN

A BLUE BIRDISH SORT OF A BIRD

A JAYISH SORT OF A BIRD

A CARDINALISH SORT OF A BIRD

A ROBINISH SORT OF A BIRD

BROWN

A CROWISH SORT OF A BIRD

A WOODPECKERISH SORT OF A BIRD

THE PEANUT GALLERY

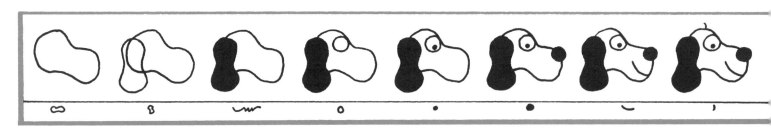

TWO WAYS TO DRAW A PEANUT.

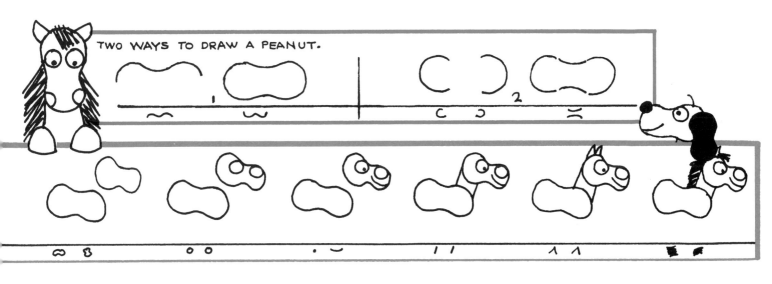

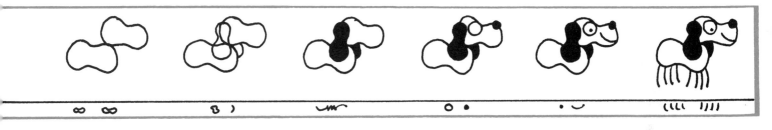

RUNNING

RABBITS!

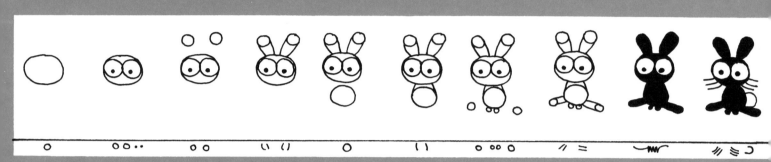

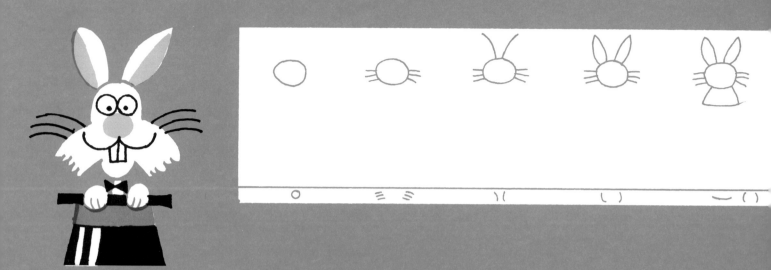

ALSO

ALSO

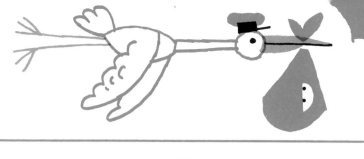

THE STORK

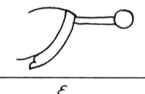  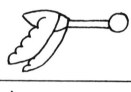

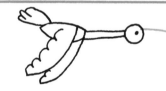 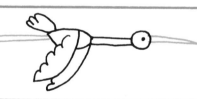 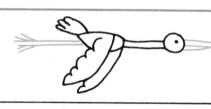

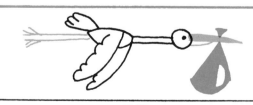 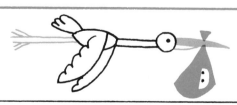 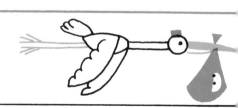

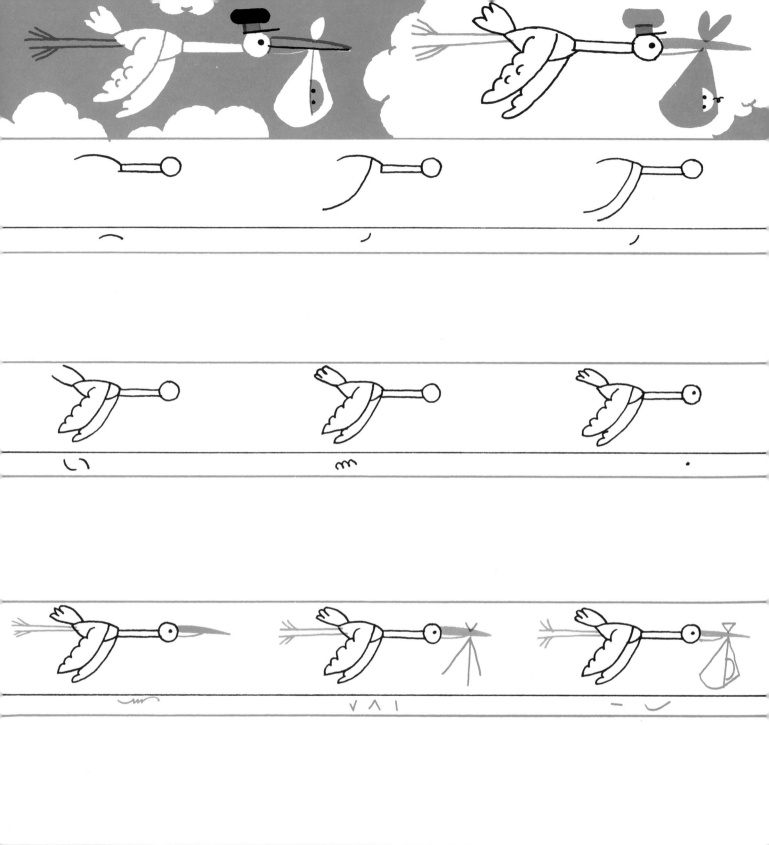

WALRUS

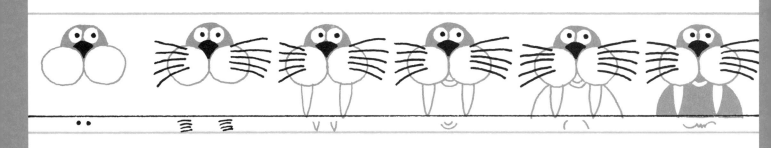

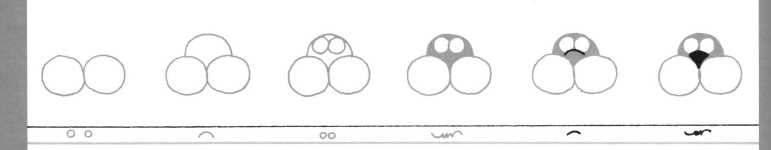

WINKING   SLEEPY   SUNGLASSES   HAT AND TIE

BEAVERS

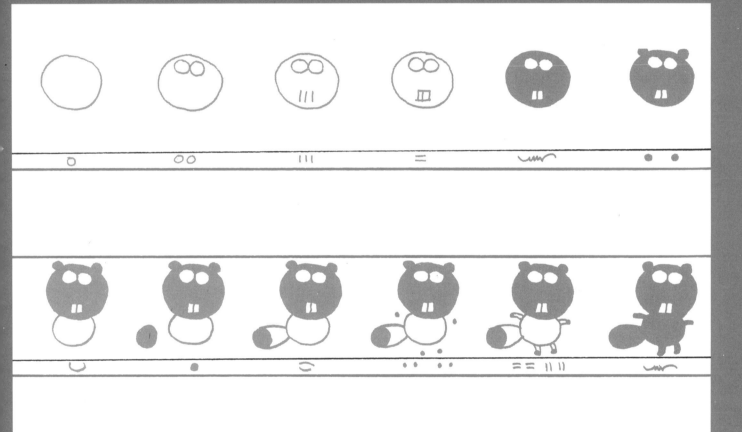

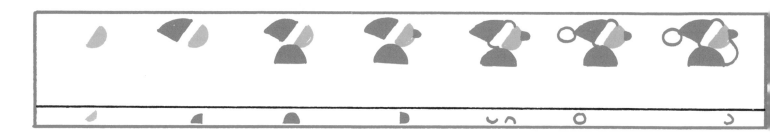

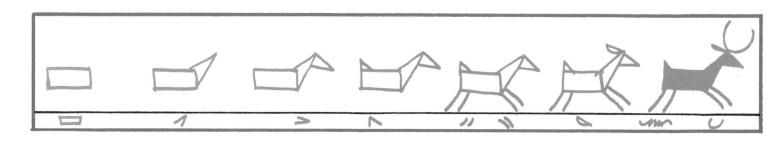

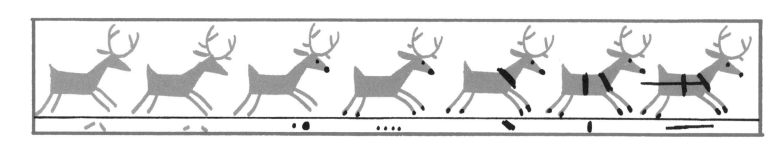

RED and GREEN

Just-right colors for
drawing Santa Claus
and Christmas trees.

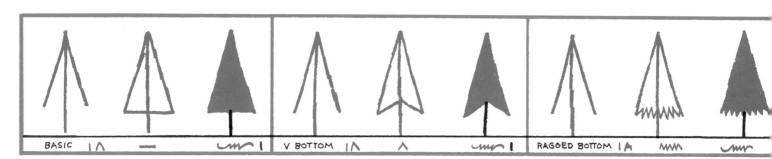

BASIC

V BOTTOM

RAGGED BOTTOM

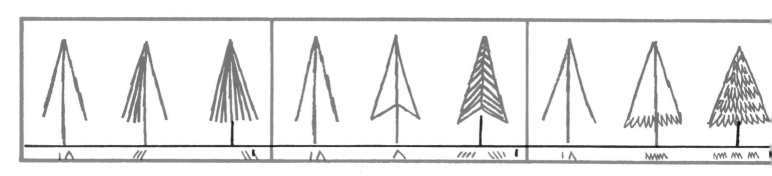

ALSO

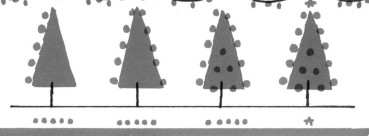

HERE ARE A FEW SIMPLE TREES
FOR YOU TO DRAW AND DECORATE.

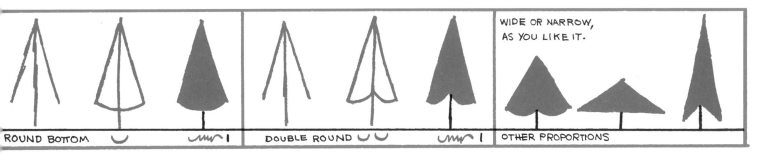

ROUND BOTTOM

DOUBLE ROUND

WIDE OR NARROW, AS YOU LIKE IT.

OTHER PROPORTIONS

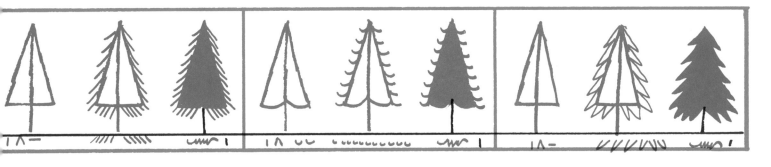

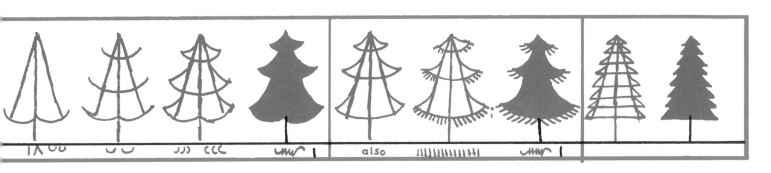

also

69

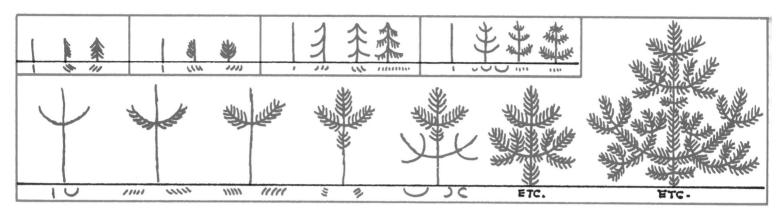

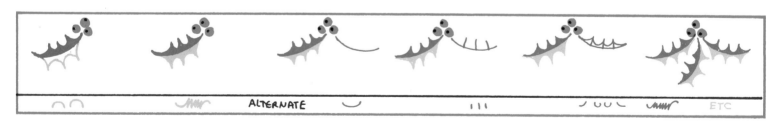

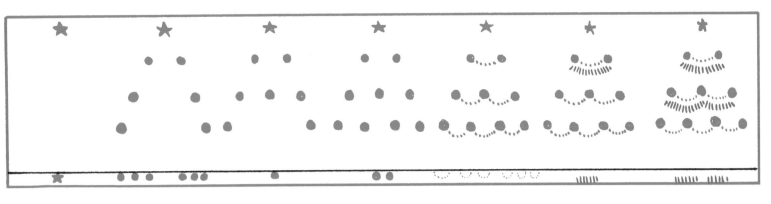

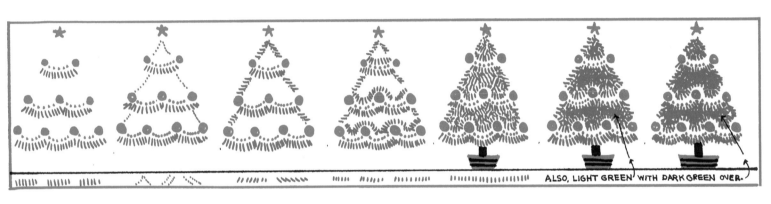

ALSO, LIGHT GREEN WITH DARK GREEN OVER.

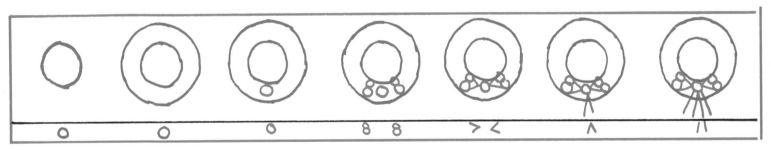

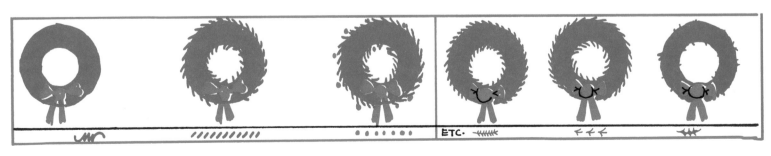

ETC.

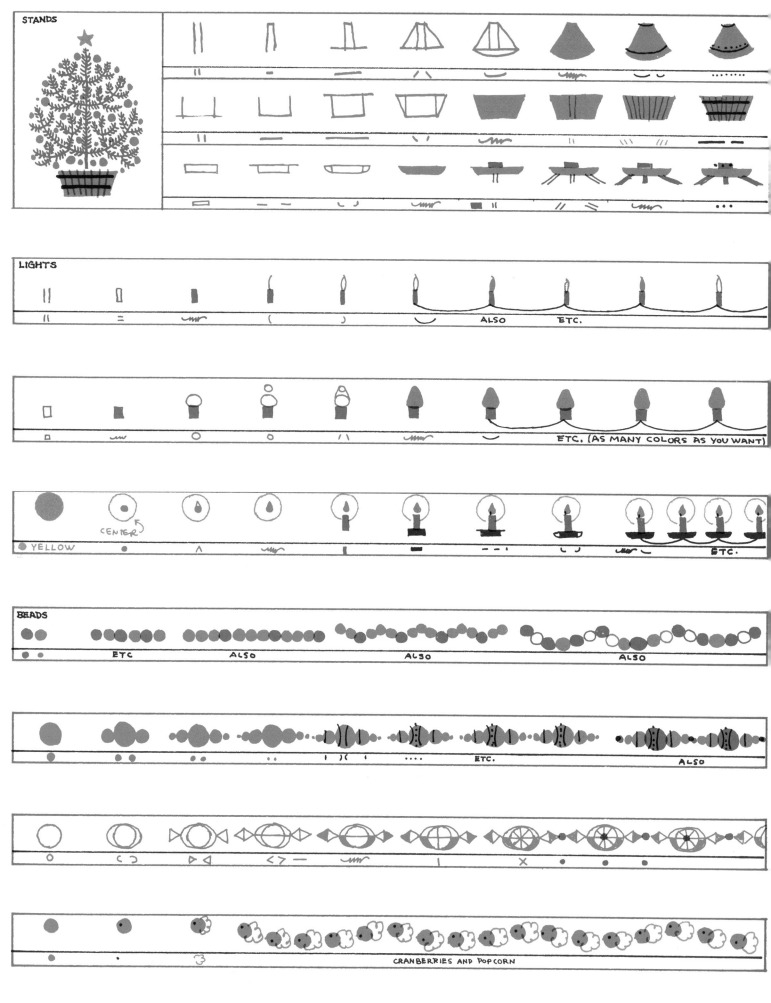

STANDS

LIGHTS

CENTER

YELLOW

BEADS

CRANBERRIES AND POPCORN

STAR-5 POINTS

O /|\\   ∧   ⊂ ⊃   ∪ ∪   O +

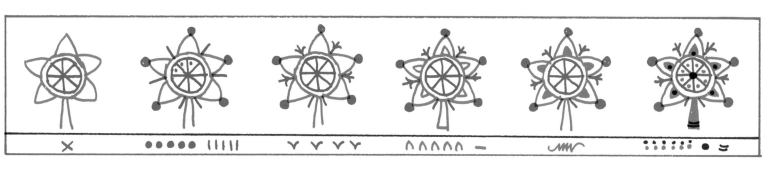

✕ ●●●●● ||||| Y Y Y Y ∧∧∧∧∧ — ∿ •:•:•:• ● ⌇

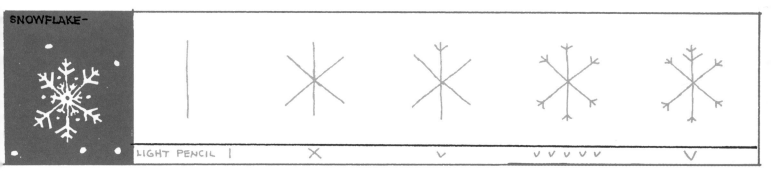

SNOWFLAKE-

LIGHT PENCIL | ✕ ∨ ∨ ∨ ∨ ∨ ∨ ∨

∨ ∨ ∨ ∨ ∨ | | | | | | ∨ ∨ ∨ ∨ ∨ •····· OUTLINE — FILL IN ∿ ERASE PENCIL ✐

DECORATIONS

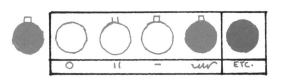
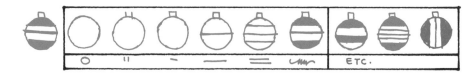

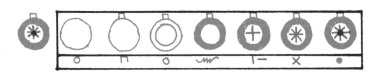
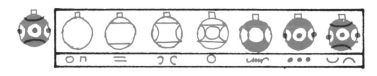

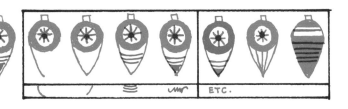
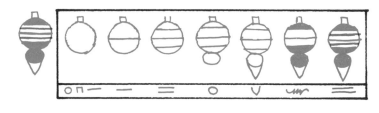

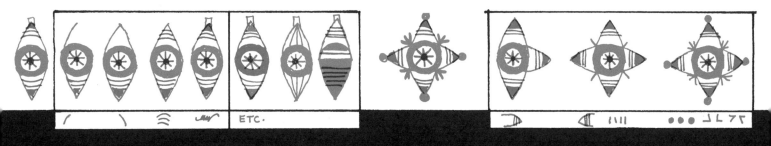

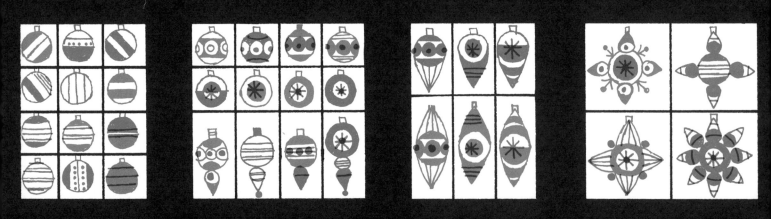

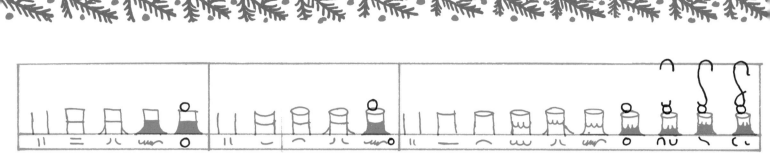

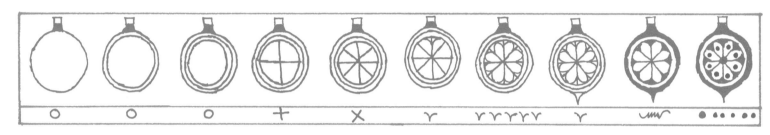

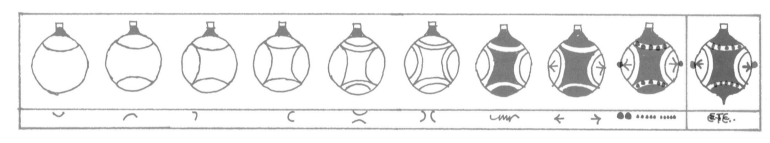

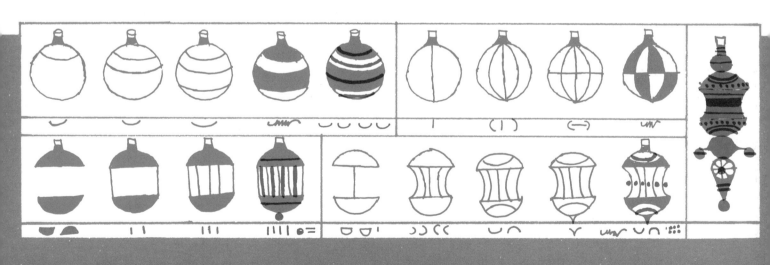

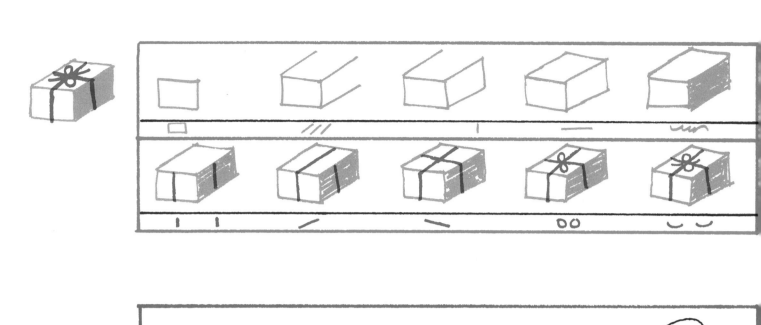

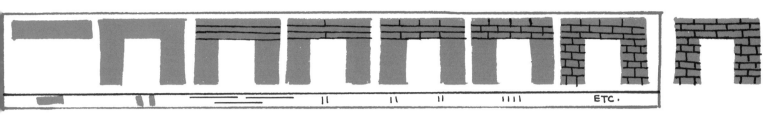

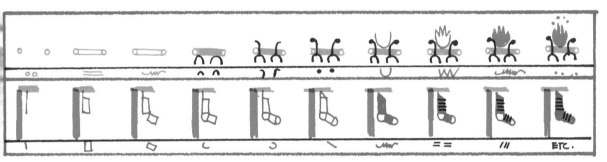

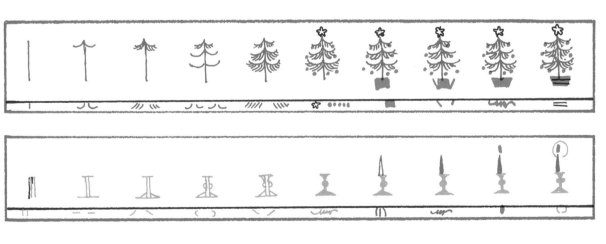

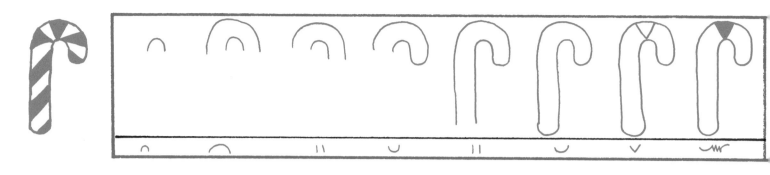

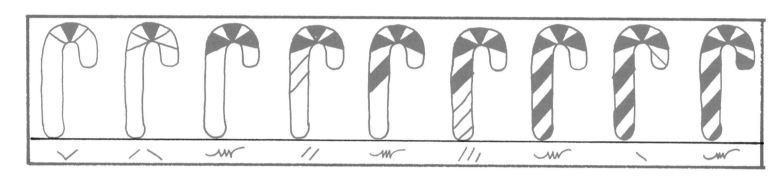

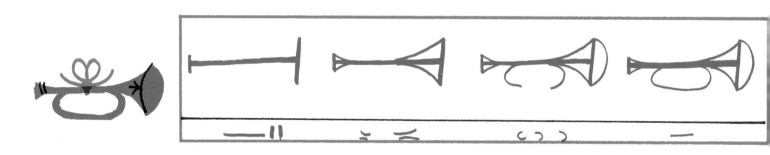

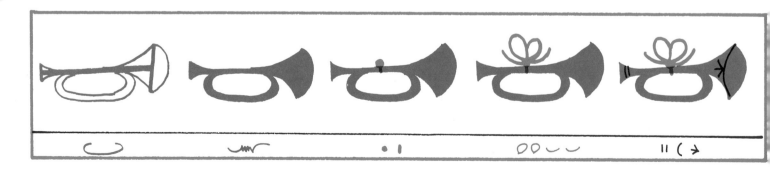

yellow

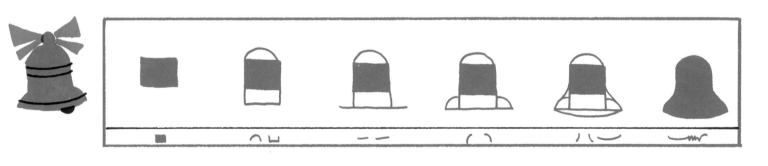

ALSO   ALSO   ALSO

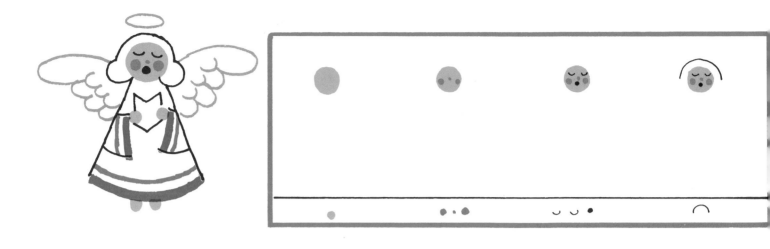

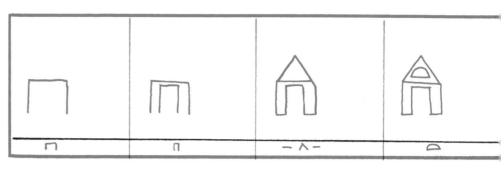

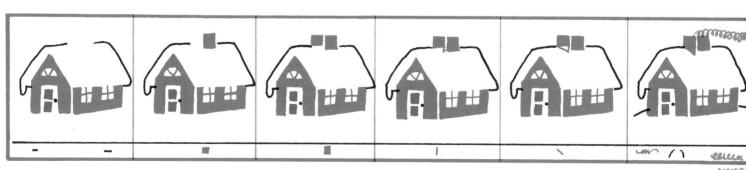

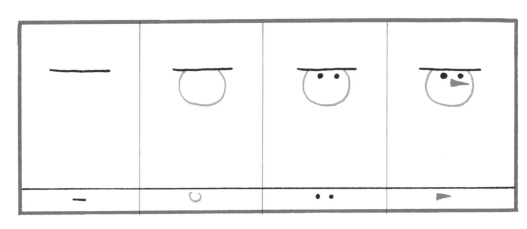

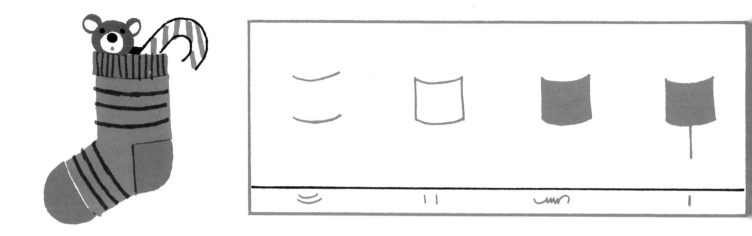

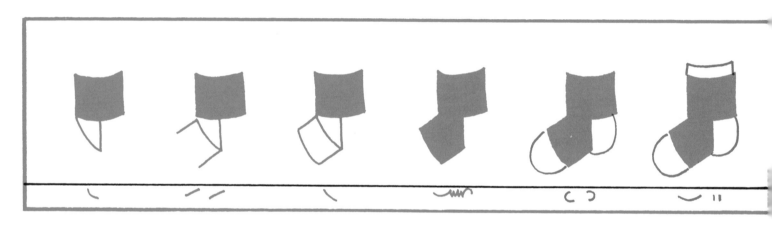

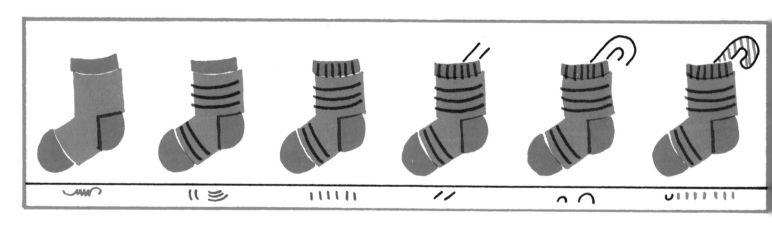

TO MAKE THIS BEAR LOOK FUZZY, I USED A DOTTED LINE

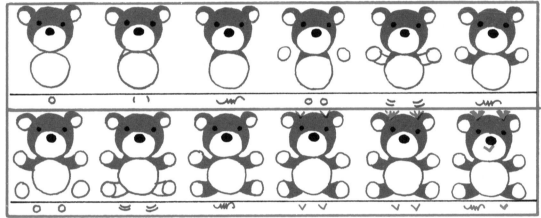

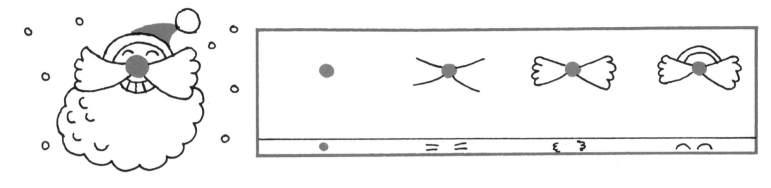

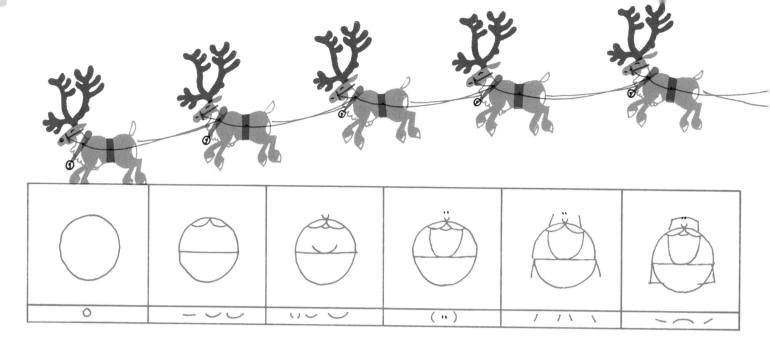

ALSO... AND ETC...

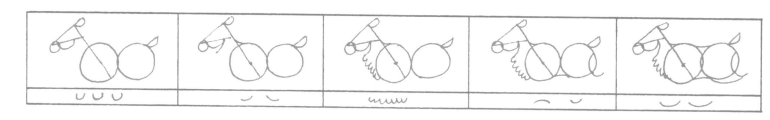

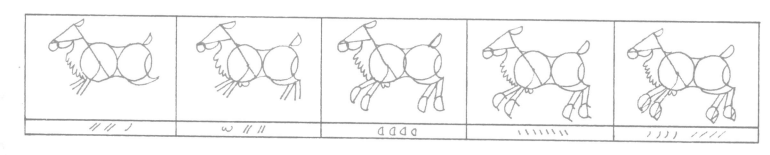

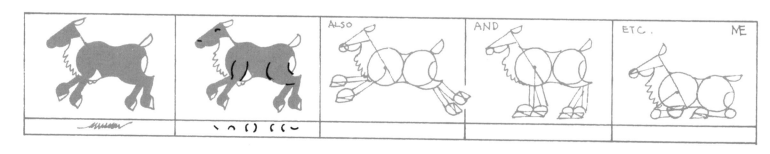

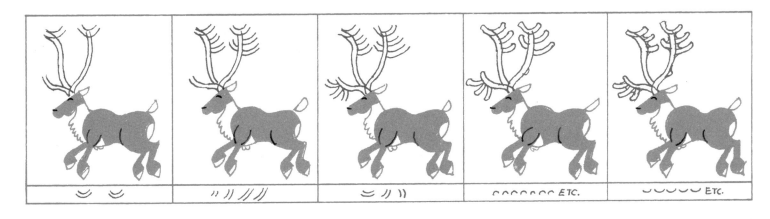

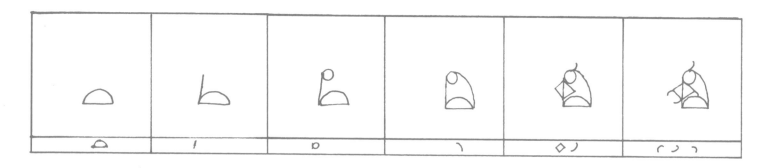

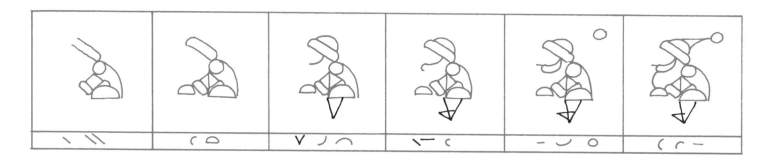

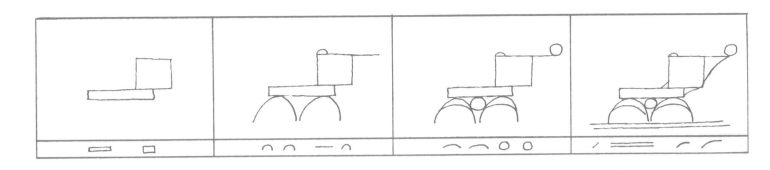

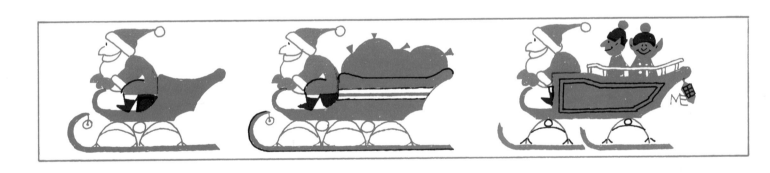

EMBERLEY FAMILY TRIVIA
FATHER — ED DREW THE PICTURES
DAUGHTER — REBECCA DREW THE INSTRUCTIONS

SON — MICHAEL, GUEST ARTIST (LOOK FOR HIS MARK ME)

GRANDDAUGHTER — ADRIANNE ENTERTAINED US ALL
DURING THE 1,000 OR SO HOURS IT
TOOK TO FINISH THIS BIG RED DRAWING BOOK